CW01082696

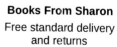

Who's Afraid of™

Clear English?

The best style is the style you don't notice.

W. Somerset Maugham

Editors: Caroline Coleman, Stephen Haynes
Editorial assistant: Mark Williams

Published in Great Britain in MMXIV by
Book House, an imprint of
The Salariya Book Company Ltd
25 Marlborough Place, Brighton BN1 1UB
www.salariya.com
www.book-house.co.uk

HB ISBN-13: 978-1-909645-81-3

1 3 5 7 9 8 6 4 2

A CIP catalogue record for this book is available
from the British Library.
Printed and bound in China.
Printed on paper from sustainable sources.

Visit
www.salariya.com
for our online catalogue and
free interactive web books.

Who's Afraid of Clear English?™

It's unclear war!

David Arscott

BOOK HOUSE
a SALARIYA imprint

People think I can teach them style. What stuff it all is! Have something to say, and say it as clearly as you can. That is the only secret.

Matthew Arnold

Any fool can make things bigger, more complex, and more violent. It takes a touch of genius and a lot of courage to move in the opposite direction.

Albert Einstein

The best sentence? The shortest.

Anatole France

The most valuable of all talents is that of never using two words when one will do.

Thomas Jefferson

Think like a wise man but communicate in the language of the people.

W. B. Yeats

Contents

Preface

*I*N A TEXT to a friend you may believe that you can write however you like – but will your message get across? We've all been involved in horrible misunderstandings which result from a clumsy use of words. Good heavens, that wasn't what you meant to suggest at all!

Aside from personal relationships, there are many other situations – such as applying for a job, or writing an essay or report – where you need to make a good impression on others. Two things are vital in these circumstances: using appropriate language and making your meaning crystal clear. This book, along with others in the series, will help you to write in a way that teachers, employers and people in authority will approve of.

Introduction

Fit for purpose

FOR TOO MANY people the idea of writing common-or-garden English similar to the way we speak is a sign of weakness. We'll come across many examples in these pages of language dressed up either to show off or to confuse, but the quotes at the front of the book make an excellent starting point. Many of our finest writers have stressed the virtue of keeping things simple, and that's the very first lesson for anyone anxious about putting words on the page in the right order.

The second lesson is that if you want to write clear English you have to think clearly in the first place. You shouldn't imagine that words will magically come to the rescue if you don't really know what you want to say.

7

Much as we champion no-nonsense English, we're certainly not arguing for a primary school level of expression. The tone of what you write – otherwise known as the 'register' – should be suitable for your intended recipient, so let's clear the air by listing a few things we're *not* against in their proper place:

- **Long words.** We'll find plenty of reasons later for preferring short ones, but you wouldn't expect to read a philosophical treatise without the need to look up a word or three in the dictionary. It's a matter of horses for courses.

- **Jargon.** Strictly for consenting adults in private. It saves time for people in the same jobs to use what amounts to professional shorthand – but keep it out of anything you write for a general readership.

It's no-go the NGO

What's an NGO? If you need to look it up, we'll save you the time: it means Non-Governmental Organisation. Any the wiser? This is just the kind of jargon businessmen and politicians spout in public every day, prompting most of us to mentally switch off. Know your audience!

- **Poetic inspiration.** Many of us enjoy literary flights of fancy. Just remember that readers happy to unravel the rich subtleties of a Shakespearian sonnet are unlikely to extend that indulgence to your own humble offering.

In short, we're assuming that you're looking for tips on writing effective, practical English, and we'll be giving you templates to cover a range of likely situations. If writing doesn't come easily to you, remember that you've been speaking the language since you were a toddler. All you have to do now is transfer that skill to the page.

Pedant alert!

Look out for the **PET PEEVE** symbol. There is a certain kind of person (language experts call them *peevologists*) who just loves to find fault with other people's use of language. 'Pet peeves' are particular mistakes (or so-called mistakes) which cause these people to get particularly aeriated and write letters to the press beginning, 'Sir, Am I alone in thinking . . . ?'

This book is not meant to turn you into a peevologist yourself – perish the thought – but it could help you to avoid needlessly provoking such people.

Follow the hacks

If you're about to write a report for the first time, there's no better place to turn for guidance than a newspaper article. The papers all have their own individual styles and target readers, of course, but two common features of a news story are clarity of expression and a step-by-step unfolding of events.

Note how the journalist typically gives you the gist of the story in the very first sentence. You'll find it a good discipline to decide at the outset what fact or idea you think is most important for your readers to know.

Now take your report forward in stages, just as a newshound does. Each paragraph should provide a little more information, perhaps backed up with quotes or useful statistics.

And the language you use? Observe how even the 'posh' papers use difficult or technical words only when nothing else will do — and then they'll often explain them to make sure the average reader doesn't give up and turn the page. If the people you're writing for have to puzzle out your meaning they'll almost certainly find better things to do than stick with you.

Smoked-glass words

It's been estimated that there are about a quarter of a million words in the English language, making it one of the richest on the planet. This means you often have a choice between two or more which have roughly the same meaning. How do you decide which is best?

Let's begin with the briefest of history lessons. Way back in the 5th century AD, land-hungry Anglo-Saxons began to swarm into Britain, and before very long their Germanic language had taken root here. It's still the basis of the tongue we speak today.

To read an Old English text you'll need a handy crib and quite a bit of patience, but you'll immediately recognise many of the words as similar or identical to those we use all these centuries later. Those forebears of ours spoke their equivalents of *I* and *me*, *he* and *his*, *we*, *our* and *us*, and we still refer to many of our activities (*to be, to love, to sing* and so on) in practically the same way as they did.

11

That keyboard test which includes every letter of the alphabet, *The quick brown fox jumps over the lazy dog*, has the vigour and briskness of Anglo-Saxon speech, although we have to admit that *jumps* and *dog* came later (Alfred the Great and his friends preferred *hound*).

Now fast-forward to 1066 and the Norman invasion. It wasn't only an abundance of French words that began to infiltrate the language but a vast new set of Latin terms, many of them used for legal and administrative business.

Administrative – that's a typical Latinate word, and we grant that it can be a very useful one. It's also, however, what we like to call a 'smoked-glass' word, as in those stretch limousines with darkened windows. For instance, in using the term *administrative adjustments* (two Latinate words together), the people inside the limousine – that is, those using the phrase – no doubt have a pretty good idea what they're referring to. Those on the outside – the rest of us – only have the cloudiest notion. We get the drift, but what exactly is going on? Please tell us!

In his 1946 essay 'Politics and the English Language', George Orwell had great fun trashing Latinate pomposity.

First he quoted a verse, striking in its simplicity, from *Ecclesiastes* in the Bible:

> *I returned and saw under the sun, that the race is not to the swift, nor the battle to the strong, neither yet bread to the wise, nor yet riches to men of understanding, nor yet favour to men of skill; but time and chance happeneth to them all.*

He then interpreted it in an idiom all too familiar today – one issuing from the dead hand of officialdom:

Pet peeve

> *Objective considerations of contemporary phenomena compel the conclusion that success or failure in competitive activities exhibits no tendency to be commensurate with innate capacity, but that a considerable element of the unpredictable must invariably be taken into account.*

Each one of those words above has a describable meaning, and the meaning of the sentence as a whole can indeed be disentangled, but the smoked-glass effect is overpowering. Our eyes glaze over and we see nothing.

Clear English motto: If you catch yourself purring smugly over the use of a grand word, immediately look for a simpler one.

13

But it's not only the long, polysyllabic words that people use in order to seem 'proper' or important. How many times have you read about something *commencing* rather than *starting* or *beginning*? And how often have you heard that something has been *utilised* rather than *used*?

The trick is to consider whether you would use the words at home. *Shall I commence my breakfast now? Should I utilise this spoon?* No? Then keep them out of what you write.

The persons on the bus

Public announcements often have a language of their own. Get on a bus and you'll probably see a sign reading something like 'A maximum of 15 persons may stand on the lower deck'.

What is this plural 'persons' doing here? Have you ever said to anyone, 'Look at those persons over there'? No, of course you haven't! We talk about one person and two or more people.

Don't let your writing become infected with a false diction as if this somehow makes it important. In fact it's nothing short of ridiculous.

14

Here are a few more tiresome temptations and their simple alternatives:

additional	extra
advise	tell
complete (a form)	fill in
comply with	keep to
convene	meet
detect	find
ensure	make sure
forward	send
in excess of	more than
in proximity to	near
in the event of	if
particulars	details
per annum	a year
prior to	before
property	house/flat
purchase	buy
terminate	end
therefore	so

Pet peeve

And a word about archaisms. Amateur writers are prone to write *whilst* for *while* and *amongst* for *among*. Today this is the equivalent of lifting the little finger when drinking a cup of tea.

Clear English motto: Don't be precious and don't show off.

15

The Hemingway principle

We all know what it's like listening to boring colleagues or relatives relating a seemingly endless story and asking ourselves whether they will ever reach the point they're trying to make. Your writing will be like that unless you get a firm grip of its structure – what journalists call 'the who, what, where and why'. That structure depends in turn upon a firm grip of the sentences you write. If they run on for several lines, with diversions from the main thread of your argument, you're likely to confuse the reader – and perhaps even yourself.

Here's a paragraph from *The Golden Bowl* by Henry James:

> The spectator of whom they would thus well have been worthy might have read meanings of his own into the intensity of their communion – or indeed, even without meanings, have found his account, aesthetically, in some gratified play of our modern sense of type, so scantly to be distinguished from our modern sense of beauty.

Contrast that with a passage from *A Moveable Feast* by Ernest Hemingway:

> By then I knew that everything good and bad left an emptiness when it stopped. But if it was bad, the emptiness filled up by itself. If it was good you could only fill it by finding something better.

We're certainly not arguing that James is the lesser writer, but Hemingway is without doubt a better model for anyone new to the task of writing clear, unambiguous English. While James is a master of the slowly unravelling sentences in which he specialises, twisting and turning his argument as he goes, Hemingway typically proceeds step by simple step.

Clear English motto: Keep it simple.

But what *is* a sentence? If you get this wrong you'll be put in the proverbial stocks by the peevologists, so it's important to understand where to stop and start again.

All regular sentences have a verb – what some helpful teachers call a 'doing word' – and they have someone or something leading the action:

The shark attacked.

In that sentence *the shark* is the subject and *attacked* is the verb. We could throw in an object, in this case its intended victim:

The shark attacked the swimmer.

We could also describe the subject and object:

The man-eating shark attacked the terrified swimmer.

And how about a bit of scene-setting?

The man-eating shark, threshing violently in the waves, attacked the terrified swimmer, who had foolishly ignored the advice of the beach lifeguards.

This is still a single sentence because it has the one central action. (The threshing and ignoring are in subsidiary, describing clauses.) But now we want to enter the mind of the swimmer:

He feared for his life.

This is not only unsurprising but faultless. We have another complete sentence with its verb. What you must never do is run two sentences together with only a comma between them.

This is considered horribly incorrect:

Pet peeve

> The shark attacked the swimmer, he feared for his life.

These are two separate sentences (each with its own verb) and, as in the Hemingway example, there should be a full stop between the two and a capital letter at the start of the second sentence:

> The shark attacked the swimmer. He feared for his life.

Of course, your writing would be tediously

Send in the paras

Once you've mastered the construction of simple sentences you'll start to wonder how many you should group together before you start a new paragraph. This time the role model is not *a popular daily newspaper, where you'll often find each sentence standing alone for ease of reading in narrow columns. Turn instead to a book in which the author develops a series of arguments.*

You'll find that each cluster of sentences deals with a distinct train of thought. When the author changes direction, however slightly, it's time to mark the event with the creation of a new paragraph.

staccato if you could never link sentences together, so here's the good news: you can use little grabbers (*and, but, because, although* and plenty more) known as 'conjunctions':

> The shark attacked the swimmer and he feared for his life.

The occasional longer sentence among short ones gives a pleasant variety to what you write, but think of yourself as a novice swimmer and make sure never to venture out of your depth.

Commonly wrong

A mishandling of fewer *and* less *will show you up in peevish eyes, so it's worth learning the difference.*

Fewer *deals with numbers — it refers to individual items that you can count, such as people or oranges.* Less *refers to the amount of a substance, such as time, oxygen or experience — you can have more or less of these things, but you can't line them up and count them. If you have* fewer *apples in your basket you'll have* less *weight to carry. Always* fewer *things,* less *stuff.*

If you remember your chemistry lessons at school, you'll know that the way to write up an experiment was something like this: 'A pipette was filled with prussic acid, and two drops were added to the beaker.'

Goodness knows what happened next, but the point is that you were writing in the 'passive voice'. Something had happened to the pipette and the drops, but there was no mention of anyone actually doing it.

You could have written 'I filled a pipette with prussic acid . . .' (the 'active voice'), but you can perhaps appreciate why the teacher would have objected to it. The outcome of the experiment was nothing to do with *you*. Anyone could have handled the materials in the same way and the result would have been the same. That's science.

A good procedure for the lab, however, is generally an undesirable one elsewhere. The passive voice is impersonal, bland, deadening.

Here are a few examples of the 'passive speak' we find all around us, with livelier 'active' alternatives beneath:

A report has been commissioned into the problems faced by our suppliers.
We have commissioned a report into the problems our suppliers face.

All our rail services have been suspended because of industrial action by drivers.
We have suspended all our rail services because the drivers have gone on strike.

You are invited to our party on Sunday, when a special anniversary cake will be cut.
We'd like to invite you to our party on Sunday, when we'll cut a special anniversary cake.

The passive, we should stress, isn't wrong – it's merely that too much of it produces a flattening effect on what you write. But there are occasions on which it is either inevitable or even preferable.

In essays, for instance, a tutor may well recommend the kind of non-personal approach favoured in the laboratory: *Hamlet is thus regarded as a typical mixed-up loner.*

The potential difficulty here is that it may lead to confusion as to whether Hamlet's condition is so regarded by the academic fraternity or by you personally as the author of the essay. Be aware of the possible need to clarify this.

Here's a halfway house:

> He was admitted to hospital after being run over by a car.
> *He was admitted to hospital after a car ran over him.*

We probably don't know who took him to the hospital, and it's irrelevant in any case, so a passive–active mix does the job very well.

And then there's what might be described either as tact or regrettable mealy-mouthed behaviour. Which of these would you choose?

> It has come to our attention that the freezer was switched off, ruining all the food.
> *We are aware that someone switched off the freezer, ruining all the food.*

The information may be the same, but the second version has an element of threat about it, with the culprit perhaps about to be exposed. The passive can be a calmer of passions!

Commonly wrong

Here are three pairs of words which frequently (see facing page) upset the apple cart.

Disinterested/uninterested

To be uninterested *is to be bored. To be* disinterested *is to be impartial, a meaning it would be sad for the English language to use. A judge or a football referee should certainly find the case or match interesting, but only as a* disinterested *party, with nothing to gain from the result.*

Flaunt/flout

To flaunt *is to show something off: 'She flaunted her wealth by parking two sports cars in the drive.' To* flout *is to disobey a code: 'He flouted the golf club rules by wearing sandals, a beret and bermuda shorts.'*

Imply/infer

We draw an inference from what someone seems to be implying. I may imply *that you're an idiot by shaking my head at what you say. You in turn notice the gesture and* infer *that I have a low opinion of you. Your angry complaint should therefore be, 'What are you implying?', not 'What are you inferring?'*

Like a sore thumb

Clichés, they say, should be avoided like the plague. They're beyond the pale and stick out in your writing like a sore thumb. Well, there are three examples for you to be going along with – and the language is riddled with so many of these hackneyed, second-hand phrases that we often use them without realising how formulaic they are.

If you want your writing to be as clear as a bell, the acid test is to take the bull by the horns, cut to the chase, knuckle down, cut through the verbiage like a knife through butter and, when push comes to shove (and although the road to hell is paved with good intentions and to err is human), try to think outside the box. That's ten more, and there we'll stop!

Using clichés is not only lazy, but may be a bar to clear thought. After all, it's easier to damn someone you dislike as, say, a Johnny-come-lately or a stuffed shirt than to explain in detail what it is you find objectionable about them.

25

The worst fault of all, because it arouses mirth rather than boredom, is that unthinking collision of clichés which produces a 'mixed metaphor'.

These gaffes are easy to make precisely because all vitality has disappeared from the original turns of phrase. If you call someone a lucky dog you probably have no mental picture of a wagging tail. Now tell him that he's skating on thin ice and you – or someone else – will crease up at the mental image you've provided.

A few from the archive:

> 'Let's not drop anchor when we aren't out of the woods yet.' – Stanford University president Gerhard Casper

> 'I smell a rat. I see him hovering in the air. But mark me, sir, I will nip him in the bud.' – Irish politician Boyle Roche

> 'All at once he was alone in this noisy hive with no place to roost.' – Tom Wolfe, *The Bonfire of the Vanities*

> 'It's just ham-fisted salami-slicing by the bean counters.' – Pentagon spokesman quoted in the *Wall Street Journal*

Timeworn though they are, clichés can spring into new life if given a deft twist. Here's a line combining two separate 'bridge' clichés – the one about not burning them and the other about not crossing them until you arrive:

We'll burn that bridge when we come to it.

Clear English motto: Only use clichés in order to subvert them for humorous, or telling, effect.

At the end of their tether

In 2004 that indefatigable language watchdog, the Plain English Campaign, asked its supporters in more than 70 countries throughout the world what they regarded as the most annoying clichés.

'At the end of the day' claimed top spot, with 'at this moment in time' and the use of 'like' as a form of punctuation sharing second place. 'With all due respect' came fourth.

'When readers or listeners come across these tired expressions,' a spokesman said, 'they start tuning out and completely miss the message – assuming there is one.'

27

Rules to be broken

If you're a newcomer to the writing game you're probably all too aware of theorists who can't wait to tell you where you're going wrong. Now's the time to relax and discover that some of the rules in the grammar books of yesteryear are today widely regarded as groundless – chiefly because they were invented by linguists who wanted English to mimic the structure of Latin.

Split infinitives

Here's Exhibit A. An infinitive is the basic form of the verb: *to go, to see, to feel* and so on. In Latin there's no equivalent of that little 'to'. The verb 'to go', for instance, is simply *ire*.

Pet peeve

So what? you may ask with a sniff, before setting off to merrily go about more important business. Ah, but you see what we've just done in that last sentence: we've split the infinitive *to go* by putting *merrily* slap bang in the middle of it! You can't do that in Latin, so the peevologists declare you shouldn't do it in English either.

28

This is arrant nonsense, but it's so deeply ingrained that most of us brought up with the 'law' tussle with split infinitives to reassure ourselves that we've made the right decision. (Mind you, we smuggled one into the text at the foot of page 8 – did you even notice?)

What matters is the clarity and effectiveness of what you write. Look what's happening to the infinitive in these three examples:

> The condemned man was seen to slowly pace his cell.
> The condemned man was seen slowly to pace his cell.
> The condemned man was seen to pace his cell slowly.

We prefer the first. The second won't do, because it could be interpreted to mean that people took a while to realise what he was doing. The third works, but separating the verb from its adverb detracts from the power of the image. There really ought to be a verb 'to slowly pace'!

Clear English motto: Follow the clarion call of those aboard the Starship *Enterprise* and never fear to boldly go.

Stranded prepositions

Here's a sentence for you to disentangle: 'What are you clearing the flat of the girl I snuggled up to in out for?'

No, we don't recommend the construction, which exaggerates a common feature of the language we speak. Broken down, the question is 'What are you clearing the flat out for?', and the extra information is that I snuggled up in it with the owner. (My lips are sealed.)

Pet peeve

The five little words that conclude our over-the-top example are known as prepositions. English sentences often end with them – though usually no more than two at a time. What you should know, but largely ignore, is that peevologists hate the practice.

Let's compare two declarations of love:

You're the girl I want to spend my life with.
You're the girl with whom I want to spend my life.

Both are correct, and equally so, but the second is so starchily formal that most modern girls would run a mile.

The story is probably apocryphal, but Winston Churchill is supposed to have written a furious marginal note when an editor suggested getting rid of prepositions at the end of his sentences: 'This is the sort of English up with which I will not put.'

Quite so – and you'll find one of ours at the foot of page 6. Too many will make your text untidy, but that's a minor matter of aesthetics.

Clear English motto: Feel no shame about using common speech patterns in your writing.

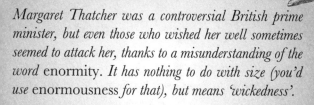

Commonly wrong

Margaret Thatcher was a controversial British prime minister, but even those who wished her well sometimes seemed to attack her, thanks to a misunderstanding of the word enormity. *It has nothing to do with size (you'd use* enormousness *for that), but means 'wickedness'.*

After her death in 2013 the US Republican leader Mitch McConnell urged the Senate, 'Let's acknowledge the enormity of what she accomplished.' That wasn't what he meant at all!

And another thing . . .

You may or may not believe the numbers, but this is what the King James Bible has to say:

> And Methuselah lived an hundred eighty and seven years, and begat Lamech. And Methuselah lived after he begat Lamech seven hundred eighty and two years, and begat sons and daughters.

Perhaps a translation from four hundred years ago isn't the most persuasive guide to English usage, but it's a useful counterweight to the 'rule' which says you shouldn't begin a sentence with *And* or *But*.

Commonly wrong

How often have you heard someone loudly protest, 'I refute the accusation!' as if that brings the argument to a close? In fact they're not refuting it at all.

To refute *something means to disprove it – in other words, to bring forward evidence to show that it's wrong. All they mean is, 'I deny it.' A very different thing!*

The short answer is that you can. We make no apologies for the *But* at the top of page 14 or the *And* near the foot of page 15. Since these words are conjunctions (their main function being to connect words, phrases and sentences), the peevologists hate to see them used in this way, but you're not being illiterate if you do.

We will concede, however, that too many of them can make your writing rather choppy – which is why we've slotted a *however* into this sentence rather than starting it with *But*.

In essays and other formal compositions you may well be encouraged to use *however* or *on the other hand* for *but*, and alternatives such as *in addition* and *moreover* for *and*. As ever, know your audience.

Where's the verb?

Pet peeve

We looked at sentences on page 17, and made the point that 'regular' ones contain a verb. Does that mean it's wrong to exclude one? The peevologists would tell you so. Sometimes, though, the verb is understood even if it doesn't show its face. Take a look at the box opposite. The punchline has a ghostly *That's* in front of it. We dropped it for dramatic effect.

33

His and her English

There was a time, not so very long ago, when you could write man to mean mankind in general, and when nobody would turn a hair if you wrote about a doctor and his patients *as if that likewise covered everyone. No longer – and that can present a problem when it comes to writing clear, correct English.*

The vogue for replacing his *with* her *is probably over (it's simply sexist in the other direction), while* a doctor and his or her patients *is a clumsy way out of the predicament, especially if a similar locution is repeated several times in the same piece. Many writers prefer* a doctor and their patients, *but we'd join the peeves in pointing out that this is horribly ungrammatical:* doctor *is singular and* their *is plural. Sorry, but it won't do.*

Turning the subject into a plural often does the trick: doctors and their patients. *Sometimes both can be singular:* Doctor and patient must agree . . . *And sometimes you'll need to reshape the entire sentence to find a way round the problem.*

Hard work? Good writing does require effort!

Addled academics

The one place where you might expect to find exemplary English is on a university campus. After all, the students are trained to think clearly, and a competent handling of the language goes hand-in-hand with that.

While the best of them certainly give their students good advice, the worst encourage a formulaic straightjacket of expression which makes the eyes glaze over. Of course a degree of formality is required: you shouldn't litter your work with personal comments or use slang, and you certainly don't write *don't*. But should you really (to take one among many examples) replace *In conclusion* with *One could draw the conclusion that*?

This is academia on its high horse, and unless your tutor threatens to deduct marks for it, you should write clear, unadulterated prose. There's a thriving educational publishing sector out there making a living from such gobbledygook, but you're not obliged to swell its profits.

Here's a selection from university guides, with everyday words followed by what they promote as preferred alternatives:

about	approximately
bad	negative
believe	assume
bring about	effect
bring up	raise
clear	evident
come from	derive from
cover up	hide
get better	improve
get worse	deteriorate
go on	continue
good	positive
idea	concept
imagine	envisage
important	significant
naturally	as one might expect
now	currently
obviously	it is quite clear that
perhaps	one could say that
problems	difficulties or issues
put together	assembled
speed up	accelerate
understand	interpret

And that's quite enough/sufficient, thank you.

36

Next we'll shudder to witness the pitiless cruelty inflicted on the English language by the business fraternity. You'll find impenetrable jargon flourishing in many a specialist field, from education to local government, but nothing beats office life for creating bombastic and self-important terminology.

Bear in mind that most of this gormless waffle has the purpose either of making the company or individual feel important – they're players in some great corporate drama – or concealing an uncomfortable truth beneath verbal camouflage.

Here's an alphabetical list, with the words and phrases interpreted into clear English as far as humanly possible. Use these phrases only if you don't mind being laughed at.

accountability matrix A list of who does what.

backfill The replacement of a sacked worker.

bandwith, not enough 'Sorry, but I haven't the time to take this job on.'

bubble up Tell someone who has more authority than you.

bucketise Sort into categories.

cascading down Passing on information from above.

challenge A relentless optimist's word for 'problem'.

circle back Agree to revisit a plan at some unspecified date.

circle the wagons Defensively bond in the face of criticism.

close of play The end of the working day.

core competency What a company does best.

Releasable issuances

We have to thank the US military rather than business for one of our favourite horrors. The Department of Defense (DoD) publishes a Writing Style Guide and Preferred Usage for DoD Issuances. *It has, we're told, unlimited* releasability. *The writing advice inside is good, so we assume that someone with low self-esteem was given the task of 'bigging it up'. Pass the Kalashnikov!*

deck A PowerPoint presentation.

decruiting Sacking people.

deep dive A fundamental change in working methods.

deep pockets Wealthy investors.

deferred success A point at which failure isn't admitted.

dehiring Sacking people.

deliverables Things to be done eventually.

demising Sacking people.

deselecting Sacking people.

diagonal slice meeting One involving staff from different teams.

dial in Include.

disambiguate Make clear.

dog and pony show A presentation regarded as worthlessly simplistic.

dog food, eating your own Using the product you've sold to a client, however bad it is.

dog in this fight, get a Make sure that we're represented.

door is open on this issue 'I'm listening.'

downsizing Sacking people.

drill down Look at the detail.

drink from the firehose To be inundated with information.

ducks, get all in a row Be organised.

flagpole, run it up the Explore an idea.

flies, see if it See if it works.

going forward From now on; at some unspecified time in the future.

granularity Detail.

grass, don't let it grow long Decide.

grow the business Make a bigger profit.

heads up Advance warning.

high-altitude view The detail comes later.

hold the ring Take responsibility.

hymn sheet, sing from the same Agree on what needs to be done.

impact (*verb*) Have an effect on.

in this space Where we are now.

incentivise Motivate.

issue (*noun*) A problem.

key (*adjective*) Important.

land and expand Sell an idea to a client and then exploit your success.

leverage (*verb*) Exploit, magnify.

long pole in the tent The hardest task.

loop, out of the Not involved.

low-hanging fruit The easiest thing to achieve.

manage expectations Prepare people for the worst.

no-brainer Something obvious.

offline In private.

open the kimono Share information.

outside-the-box thinking Imagination.

paradigm shift A significant change.

park that Save it for another day.
party, come to the Join in.
proactive Getting in first.
product evangelist A properly keen member
   of staff.
push the envelope Go to the extremes.
radar, got you on my 'I'm listening.'
revert to you Get back to you.

Commonly wrong

The word literally *means 'exactly so', or 'just as the
words indicate', and should never be used as a term of
exaggeration – unless you wish to sound ridiculous.*

*A cloned man might be literally beside himself with
amazement, and if he became depressed on a visit to a
civic amenity site (see Euphemisms, page 70), he might
be literally down in the dumps, but if he tells you that
'The guitar riff literally blew my mind away!' he can't
be speaking the truth, because after that unlikely event he
wouldn't be here to tell the tale.*

The word he's after is figuratively, *as in a figure
of speech.*

rightsizing Sacking people.

role-based pay allowance Bonus.

same page, be on the Think alike.

send over the wall Pass on to a client.

silo An individual department or 'vertical' (see below).

solutioneering Thinking.

sprinkle one's magic Work hard for the company.

storyboard, create the Outline what's going to happen.

strategic staircase Plan for the future.

sunset it Kill it off.

synergise Work as a team.

take it to the next level Go ahead.

tape, don't fight the Don't oppose market forces.

taper Cut back on.

thought leader Bright spark.

thought shower Brainstorm.

touch base Report back.

train set The company, as seen by someone who runs it.

transitioning Sacking people.

upskill Retrain to make more useful.

vanilla Boring.

vertical Distinct area of expertise.

workshop (*verb*) To tackle something.

zero-sum game Some win, some lose.

42

Pesky pitfalls

By now, we hope, your sentences have ceased to sprawl, your vocabulary is largely that of everyday speech, your text is jargon-free and you're writing mainly in the active rather than the passive voice. If so, you're well on your way – and it's time to look out for the numerous little potholes in the road ahead.

Other books in this series go into more detail on grammar, punctuation and spelling, but here's a checklist of common mistakes which, if you succumb to them, will affect the clarity and the effectiveness of your writing.

Dangling participles

Otherwise known as hanging or unattached participles, these sound painful but are more likely to produce mirth – and at your expense.

The present participle is the *-ing* version of the verb, as in *reading* and *writing*, and it loves to sit in descriptive phrases: 'Reading the novel, I wept.'

This is a faultless sentence. Who was reading the novel? I was. Now puzzle out who was reading it in this version of events:

> Reading the novel, Tess had me weeping tears of pity.

The rule about 'absolute' phrases is that they're like loners at a party who need an arm to cling to, so they seize the nearest they can find. It may be obvious that, as the heroine, Tess can't really be reading the book in which she appears, but that's what the sentence is telling us nonetheless.

Here are a couple of examples which, on reflection, you would rather not have written:

> Foul-smelling and swimming in grease, I pushed the plate away from me in disgust.

> Water-skiing in Acapulco Bay, a shark suddenly swam alongside us.

Although present participles are usually the guilty party, watch out for other 'floating' phrases just waiting to embarrass you:

> At the age of 60 the government will issue you with a free bus pass.

Yes, people will understand what you mean, and nobody would pick you up if they heard you say it, but written language requires a little more precision. You might have begun by saying *When you reach the age of 60 . . .* (a clause with its own subject and verb), but as it stands you're looking ahead to a government which has been in power for a full six decades.

When it's *its*

The biggest source of grief of them all, and even those of us who know the rule inside out will often carelessly get it wrong.

Here's the source of the problem: an apostrophe is commonly used to denote possession, as in *Jack's pen* and *Julia's bag*. It's no surprise, then, that people write *The tree shed it's leaves* – which is, unfortunately, the wrong choice. Why? Because we need *it's* as the shortened form of *it is* and *it has*, as in *It's [it is] the first time it's [it has] been seen here.*

Let's return to our tree, which has, with the onset of winter, begun to display bare branches. Use this as your template:

It's the first time it's shed its leaves.

45

The greengrocer's apostrophe

But how many greengrocers? In this case just one, as we've placed the apostrophe directly after the singular form. More than one? Then it's *greengrocers'*.

These poor shopkeepers have earned the scorn of peevologists for their seemingly universal habit of inserting random apostrophes into their signs. Be aware that the plural of *banana* is *bananas*, and never, ever *banana's*.

Clear English motto: Take care over your apostrophes. One little mark in the wrong place can ruin your literary reputation.

Unfussy plurals

It was once common to see Members of Parliament *written as* MP's *in newspapers, but most these days prefer* MPs *as being tidier. Doing away with the apostrophe here is good practice, as long as no ugliness is involved.* CDs, Ps and Qs *and* AGMs *are fine, but some may feel that fellows of the Royal Society look better as* FRS's.

The strange verb 'to of'

Tweets, blogs and forums are awash with awful English, but there's little worse than the peppering of messages with the constructions *could of, would of* and *should of.* What on earth can they mean?

It's a question of mishearing. What the illiterate posters are mimicking is the shortened form of the verb 'to have'. The above monstrosities should be (informally) written as *could've, would've* and *should've*.

Having to agree

We're unlikely to make the mistake of writing 'I were' or 'they was', because (even if we don't think about such things) we know instinctively that singular nouns take the singular form of the verb and plurals likewise demand the plural. Once we begin constructing sentences of any length, though, it's easy to confuse the two.

See if you can spot the errors in these examples:

> The glory of Rome, as any tourist knows, are the ancient statues on every street corner.

47

A gaggle of geese were strutting around the farmyard.

Alas, we've taken our eye off the singular/plural ball. The ancient statues have tempted us into that *are*, but the subject of the sentence is actually the (singular) glory of Rome, which therefore *is* the statues. Likewise, we see the geese on parade and give them a plural *were*, whereas we're really talking about the gaggle, which is singular: it *was* strutting.

Pet peeve

Beware those crafty plurals which smuggle themselves in between commas or brackets:

The prime minister, along with some of his cabinet colleagues, were pelted by the crowd.

Wrong! The phrase 'along with some of his cabinet colleagues' is extra information and the sentence could function perfectly well without it. The gist of the story is that 'The prime minister *was* pelted by the crowd': his colleagues have (grammatically, at least) nothing to do with it. We could, however, combine them to give a genuine plural:

The prime minister and some of his cabinet colleagues were pelted by the crowd.

A few minor rules:

• *Either* and *neither* are regarded as singular when only two people or things are spoken about (*Either/neither of them* is *acceptable*) but with *neither/ nor* the verb agrees with the subject nearest to it: *Neither she nor they* eat *meat. Neither they nor he* drinks *lager*.

• *Every, everyone, everybody, nobody* and *someone* are all singular: *Every last man and woman* is *coming to the party*.

• *Each* is singular (*Each dog* wags *its tail*) except when the subject is plural (*The dogs each* wag *their tails*).

• You can choose to regard 'collective' nouns such as football teams as singular or plural – but be consistent. This is correct (both plural):

Chelsea *are* spending even more money in the hope of improving *their* league position.

This (a singular/plural mismatch) is horribly wrong:

The family *is* spending *their* Christmas at home.

In the right place

Some words have a tendency to wander into the wrong position, so making your meaning unclear – and 'only' is a regular culprit.

He has only been playing the piano for a year.

He's been doing nothing else? That seems a terrible waste of a life. Or perhaps it should be:

He has been playing the piano for only a year.

'Nearly' is another wanderer. We can't avoid such slips in everyday speech, but they glare out at you from the page.

She nearly walked as far as the cliff-edge.

Perhaps she didn't go there after all, or perhaps she went by car instead. Or:

She walked nearly as far as the cliff-edge.

That's clearer!

Sometimes words impeccably in the right order will nevertheless accidentally combine with others to create an unintended mental diversion.

50

When the gale was *blowing raspberries* and currants were torn to shreds.

It was a project costing an arm and *a leg over* which I had no control.

He saw a girl blonde and *rosy-cheeked behind* the shop counter.

Clear English motto: However easily your writing flows, always read it over carefully before you send it out into the world.

Me, myself and I

A strange use of myself *seems to go hand-in-hand with pompous management-speak. You'll hear someone say 'Myself and the team will do it' or 'Just forward it to myself'. Both are wrong. You can use the word as an intensifier ('I don't like cheese myself, but you're welcome to it') or reflexively (that's what it's called when you do something to yourself: 'I've cut myself with the cheese knife'), but the ordinary subject and object forms are, of course,* I *and* me.

Just ask Mr Pompous, 'Will yourself do it?' and he'll perhaps realise how stupid he sounds.

Not to like

In common parlance *like* is often used for *as* or *as if* in such sentences as *She can't reach the high notes like she used to* and *He drove madly like there was no tomorrow*. The error looks even worse in print.

Commonly wrong

The words lay *and* lie *are very often confused. Hens, as we know, lay eggs, so if you tell us 'I lay on the floor every morning when I do my exercises' we're tempted to imagine you clucking away too. What you presumably mean to say is 'I lie on the floor.'*

The nub of the problem is that we have three distinct verbs here: to lay, to lie *(down) and* to lie *(dishonestly).*

I lay *flooring for a living, I* laid *some yesterday and I shall be* laying *it again tomorrow.*

I lie *(down) today, I* lay *in my bed last night and I shall be* lying *in it again tonight.*

I lie *(dishonestly) today, I* lied *to you yesterday and (forgive me) I shall be* lying *to you again tomorrow.*

Use *like* for comparisons:

> He has a face *like* a melon.
> I've been working *like* a dog.

(Note that you'd be working *as* a dog only if you meant you were performing its functions. As a guard dog, perhaps?)

But use *as* when you mean 'in the same way as':

> She can't reach the high notes as she used to.
> He drove madly *as if* there was no tomorrow.

(It's even better if you write 'As if there *were* no tomorrow'. You can look up 'subjunctive' in the companion volume on grammar.)

When might is right

The words *may* and *might* aren't interchangeable, but even native speakers get them muddled. First consider these two sentences:

> *I may* go to the cinema today.
> Yesterday I thought *I might* go to the cinema.

That's a simple change from present to past.

But now here's *might* used in the present tense, to suggest something highly unlikely:

Pigs might fly.

Everyone realises that you don't expect it to happen, whereas if you wrote *Pigs may fly* they would probably question your sanity.

Here are two more uses of this maddeningly troublesome pair:

I may have done it. (It's possible, but I don't know or can't remember.)

I might have done it. (But the fact is that I didn't.)

Pet peeve

The most common errors occur in the past tense, in sentences such as this:

If Ann Boleyn had produced a male heir, Henry VIII may not have had her executed.

What's wrong here is that *may* suggests doubt or possibility, whereas we know full well that Henry did indeed carry out the foul deed – although he *might* not have done it in other circumstances.

Quicker, quickly

We don't wish to be too technical, but *quicker* and *slower* are adjectives, describing a noun, whereas *quickly* and *slowly* are their matching adverbs, describing a verb. The adjectives generally cause no problems:

> The *slower* tortoise proverbially beats the *quicker* hare.

The adverbs, though, are often abused, like this:

> The hare ran *quicker* than the tortoise.

No, no, that won't do. Let's try again . . .

> The hare ran *more quickly* than the tortoise, which hobbled *slowly* along.

Much better!

Ugly usage

We're used to problems regarding the past tense of *use to*. Given the choice between *Didn't use to* and *Used not to* we'd plump heavily for the latter. What's unforgiveable is to write *Didn't used to*. 'Didn't used'? It's simply barbaric.

55

And a few more . . .

• *Centred around*: Things are centred *on* a fixed point, not *around* it.

• *Try and*: We're all guilty of this usage in day-to-day conversation, but we should try to do rather better when we write: *Let's try to see one another on Sunday.*

• *The reason is because:* An error of logic, since the reason for something can't be caused by anything else. *The reason for sending you a bunch of roses is that I love you madly.*

• *Those kind of thing:* There's a mismatch here (*see page 47*) between the plural *those* and the single *kind* – Those kinds *of rose are delightful, but I'm afraid* this kind *of gift isn't enough to win my heart.*

• *Irony:* Be careful how you use this word – and if in doubt, don't use it at all! The singer Alanis Morissette, in her song 'Ironic', equates it with 'rain on your wedding day . . . a free ride when you've already paid'. No, that's just rotten luck. Irony, to grossly simplify a shifty rhetorical device, is a clash between appearance and reality: the Ancient Mariner's 'Water, water, every where, | Nor any drop to drink.'

Now that you're ready to begin writing, you need to concern yourself with how to organise the words on the page.

There are so many possible variations in matters of punctuation, the abbreviation of words, their capitalisation, even occasionally of spelling, that newspapers and publishing houses have produced style guides for their editors and sub-editors. Some of these are now on sale to the public, and we suggest that you have one to hand for those moments when you find making a choice too stressful.

Punctuation

This series includes a separate guide to this thorny subject, but our advice to the beginner is to make do with only a small range of the useful little marks, dots and squiggles on offer. Forget, for instance, the semicolon (;). Few people know how to use it properly; save it for later.

Commonly wrong

Some words have been so contaminated by repeated error that purists may soon have to admit defeat.

To decimate *something is to reduce it by a tenth, not (or certainly not originally) to smash it to pieces. The Roman army would punish a mutinous legion by putting ten per cent of its soldiers to death, so decimating it.*

A bruise is typically livid, *or black and blue. Somehow the colour has become synonymous with feelings of rage.*

Chronic *doesn't mean awful or painful, but long-lasting or frequently recurring, as in certain medical conditions.*

We can deny *something without necessarily being in* denial – *a phrase with specific psychological connotations.*

As for exponential growth, *it doesn't mean 'incredibly fast' or 'unstoppable'. What it* does *mean you'll have to look up in a maths textbook – and we respectfully advise the same before you tackle those equally dangerous twin concepts,* lowest common denominator *and* highest common factor. *Tread carefully!*

Commas: These are your footsoldiers. We've already forbidden (page 19) their use between two separate sentences – but they're invaluable for organising your text line by line.

Very often they orchestrate the rhythms of ordinary speech, and that's a good place to begin:

> I'm getting the hang of this writing game, but I've not finished learning yet.

Read that aloud to yourself and you'll realise that the comma marks a very brief natural pause, and you may even have taken a breath there.

A comma is also useful if the opening phrase is a kind of preamble to the main business of the sentence:

> Long before he was crowned, Richard the Lionheart had made a name for himself as a warrior.

Note that it also avoids confusion in this case. If we read *Long before he was crowned Richard,* we might expect the rest of the sentence to tell us that he had been christened with another name.

And here's another example of a comma preventing ambiguity:

I didn't take part in order to annoy him.

I didn't take part, in order to annoy him.

Did he take part? In the first sentence, yes, but not with the aim of being a nuisance. In the second, no – and that *was* a provocation.

Two commas working in tandem act as brackets, separating off additional information:

Richard's reign, which lasted almost ten years, was marked chiefly by his absence on the Crusades.

But note the difference between these two sentences:

The king who burned the cakes turned out to be the saviour of his country.

The king, who burned the cakes, turned out to be the saviour of his country.

The first tells us that England's saviour was the careless monarch who took his eye off the oven.

The second assumes that we've already been talking about Alfred: the message is that he saved his country, and we're told merely in passing what he got up to in the kitchen.

Colons: Here's one of many in this book. They're useful for introducing lists or separate segments of information. In fussier days gone by they were followed by a little dash (:–), but that looks messy. In the United States a colon is usually followed by a capital letter. Here we prefer lower case. *We need three things: food, water and a roof over our heads.*

Hyphens: These are the little dashes (-) that connect compound words, and you can agonise forever over the necessity of including them. Consider the following, taken from the *Guardian* newspaper's style guide:

bric-a-brac, film-maker, first-hand, lamp-post, banknote, biannual, catchphrase, firefighter, box office, eye level, gun battle, mail train

You can be sure that a large team of journalists spent many hours debating whether a particular compound should appear in the first, second or third list above. Don't worry about the logic of it, but do aim to be consistent.

Troublesome doubles

A few echoing words, or homophones, which regularly cause confusion:

aural *(of the ear);* oral *(of the mouth)*

canvas *(tent material);* canvass *(seek votes)*

cereal *(breakfast food);* serial *(repeat)*

complement *(augment);* compliment *(praise)*

currant *(fruit);* current *(tide, voltage, happening now)*

defuse *(make harmless);* diffuse *(spread about)*

dependant *(someone receiving support);* dependent *(contingent upon)*

elicit *(draw out);* illicit *(forbidden)*

fazed *(overwhelmed);* phased *(in stages)*

incidence *(amount/rate);* incidents *(events)*

metal *(material);* mettle *(pluck)*

profit *(financial gain);* prophet *(seer)*

sight *(what can be seen);* site *(location);* cite *(produce in evidence)*

stationary *(still);* stationery *(writing materials)*

wave *(hand gesture, seawash);* waive *(relinquish)*

Plain English motto: Use a dictionary – if in doubt, seek it out.

Dashes (en-rules): Longer than hyphens, these can add vigour to your text. The danger is that you use them too frequently and give the page a harum-scarum look. Use them when you want to create something of a flourish at the end of a sentence – as at the foot of the box opposite.

Parentheses: We've seen that you can use commas to separate material off from the main business of a sentence (*The coat, a bright green, caught everyone's attention*), but sometimes the added information is rather longer and threatens to disrupt the flow of thought. Putting it between brackets helps readers make the leap from start to finish:

> The coat (a bright green double-breasted affair bought in Dublin a week before) caught everyone's attention.

You can use dashes instead of brackets, but beware the temptation to use a parenthetical pair plus a single emphatic one in the same long sentence. This gets very confusing indeed:

Pet peeve

> Nellie was delighted to visit the old house – a survivor of Civil War times – and was accompanied by her great uncle Sam – the oldest member of the family.

Rows of dots: Use them to indicate missing material in a text and, sparingly, to prepare the ground for new material...

Quotation marks: The usual practice in UK English is to use single quotes for speech, with double ones for quotes within quotes:

> 'I'm angry with mother,' she said, 'because she told me I was "a spoilt brat" and deserved what I got.'

Question marks: Their use seems obvious, but some writers have a tendency to put them at the end of any sentence which expresses doubt:

Pet peeve

> He wonders whether she may come?

We've no idea either, but the thrust of the sentence is that he's wondering. It's not a query, so the question mark shouldn't be there.

Exclamation marks: In fiction they accompany cries of pain and wonder, but it's the sign of the amateur writer to have them littering page after unremarkable page:

> And then we had a new dog! He was a true friend!

Apostrophes: We've already touched on *it's/ its* and the frailties of greengrocers, but can't avoid a little more on this touchiest of subjects.

Thanks to the use of apostrophes not only for possession (*Winston's cigars*) but to show that letters are missing (*it's* for *it is*), there's a group of all-too-similar words that's always getting people into trouble:

they're (they are)
their (belonging to them)
there (in that place)

we're (we are)
were (past tense of *are*)
where (in what place)

who's (*who is* or *who has*)
whose (belonging to whom)

you're (you are)
your (belonging to you)

Pet
peeve

And while we're issuing a warning about false echoes, never (as many bloggers painfully do) confuse *our* with *are*: *We thoroughly enjoyed are tea.* This is dreadful.

Presentation

Correct grammar and punctuation are essential, but don't ignore those other details which make your text easy on the eye.

Cramped spacing, a multiplicity of typefaces, a confusion of differently weighted headings and subheads – all of these discourage a reader from persevering with what may otherwise be an excellent piece of writing. As ever, look carefully at how the professionals do it.

Capital letters: Too many of these will give your writing a cluttered look. Beginners are tempted to 'cap up' any word which seems important:

> I visited my Solicitor in Ealing to discuss Mother's last Will and Testament, and learned that I was to come into a small Fortune overnight.

The only words that need their capital here are the first person 'I' and 'Ealing', as it's a place-name. Your 'solicitor' is a common noun, as are 'mother' (though you loved her dearly), 'will', 'testament' and 'fortune'.

If you doubt this advice, as many newcomers do, take a look at the quality daily newspapers. There was a time when they, too, would have treated some common nouns more reverently, but the modern way is to prune as many of those heavy capitals as possible.

What you'll discover is that, although the Queen is generally given special dispensation, other 'important' people, such as the prime minister, are not. As a compromise, the Archbishop of Canterbury may have his rank glorified in the first instance, but subsequent references will pare him down to 'the archbishop'.

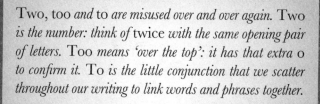

Commonly wrong

Two, too *and* to *are misused over and over again.* Two *is the number: think of* twice *with the same opening pair of letters.* Too *means 'over the top': it has that extra* o *to confirm it.* To *is the little conjunction that we scatter throughout our writing to link words and phrases together.*

He drank *two* glasses of whisky *to* drown his sorrows, but it proved *too* much for his frail constitution.

Abbreviations: The danger here is that you assume knowledge your readers don't have. In a newsletter for your own small group of enthusiasts it may be safe to write ADCS, certain that they'll recognise this as the acronym for the Afghan–Dachshund Crossbreed Society, but if there's the slightest doubt you should give the name in full when you first use it, with the initials in brackets.

> Our committee members visited the Loamshire District Health Authority (LDHA) to express our concerns. LDHA advised us not to worry.

Paragraphs: In an essay you'll probably feel obliged to proceed methodically, with sentences logically bound together; but, writing for a less demanding audience than a university don, you can break the rules in the interest of readability.

Long, unbroken wodges of text are, frankly, offputting to the general reader. As long as you're not breaking into a concentrated train of thought, feel free to create a new paragraph and let your text breathe.

Bullet points: If you have items, facts or arguments in list form, bullet points are a useful device:

- **They catch the eye and lead the reader on.**
- **They fix the main points in a nutshell.**
- **They can be as short and snappy as you wish.**
- **They help you to get your own priorities in order as you create them.**

Ideally, of course, you would have everything sorted out in your head before you began, but writing rarely works like that. Worry too much about the detail and you'll find that you never get started. Our tip is to knock out a rough draft without bothering too much about the niceties, then painstakingly improve it using the information you've gleaned from this book.

Stand by for a few sample texts, meanwhile pondering the words of the author Neil Gaiman: 'This is how you do it: you sit down at the keyboard and you put one word after another until it's done. It's that easy, and that hard.'

Euphemisms

Are we being tactful, mealy-mouthed or plain dishonest when we hide an uncomfortable fact behind a verbal mask? Rest assured that people will usually know your true meaning — an estate agent's 'delightfully cosy' is easily translated as 'stiflingly claustrophobic' — so you'll be forgiven only if your motives are pure.

Well-meaning euphemisms include varieties of 'being let go' when losing your job, and 'passing away' when bereaved. Many recipients of this emollient language must nonetheless want to cry out, 'But you're firing me!' or 'No, she's dead!'

A notably squeamish version of the practice is the renaming of council rubbish dumps, or tips, now widely known as 'civic amenity sites' — which might, to the uninitiated, suggest children's playgrounds. Horrible word, 'rubbish'!

When Japan surrendered after the Second World War, the emperor Hirohito told the nation that the war had 'developed in a way not necessarily to Japan's advantage'. Who did he think he was fooling?

Winston Churchill, on the other hand, was playing to the gallery when he once accused an opponent in the House of Commons – where it's regarded as unparliamentary language to call anyone a liar – of 'terminological inexactitude'. Point made.

Here are a few terms we have learned to distrust, along with their real meanings:

- **binocular deprivation** *Stitching up an animal's eyes for research.*
- **collateral damage** *The killing of civilians in a war.*
- **economical with the truth** *Lying.*
- **enhanced interrogation methods** *Torture.*
- **extraordinary rendition** *The illegal seizing of an individual who is then flown to another country.*
- **negative cash flow** *Broke.*
- **redacted** *(of official documents) Edited to hide evidence.*
- **spend more time with one's family** *(of a politician) Resign because of a scandal.*

Clear English motto: Everyone sees through them, so use euphemisms only for humour:

'She looked as if she had been poured into her clothes and had forgotten to say "when".' – P. G. Wodehouse

How to do it

We end with some templates designed for a variety of situations, acknowledging the obvious fact that none will exactly match your own needs. Adapt them as the spirit takes you.

A word, first, about *tone*. In this book you'll have noticed that we've been addressing you in a chatty manner throughout (and we trust that you've been happy with that). Public discourse tends to be much less formal than even a generation ago, and you don't have to be stiffly starched, well pressed and buttoned up in what you write.

Yes, the kind of language you use should reflect the seriousness of the subject matter and your relationship (if there is one) with the recipient, singular or plural. In some cases your tone will be more remote and impersonal. But, whatever the circumstances, don't stray from the fundamental rules of clear English: write as closely as you can to the spoken tongue, keeping your sentences short and your words plain.

A press release

Journalists are busy people, and they're pretty impatient, too. If you're sending them a flyer about the organisation you represent, don't use more than one side of a single sheet of paper, and don't include a lot of fussy detail. If it looks boring, they'll chuck it straight in the bin.

SCHOOL KIDS BEAT THE BOUNDS

Junior children from St Olaf's School will revive a medieval custom in May when they walk six miles round the Oakford parish boundary, beating the bushes as they go and getting thrown up into the air at regular intervals.

The ancient practice was last recorded in the village in 1543. It was a way of establishing who owned the local fields, ponds and woodland.

School head Sue Barleycorn says the idea came from a year 9 history project.

'We learned that it was a real community event,' she says. 'It was a good excuse for drinking and feasting. Young boys were tossed into the air at certain points along the route. We plan to do the same – but very gently!'

Mrs Barleycorn is hoping that large numbers of villagers will join in the fun. The children will be collecting money for their chosen charity, the local donkey sanctuary.

The Beating the Bounds ceremony takes place on Friday 13 May, starting at the church at 9 a.m.

School contact: Tom Norris, 406322.

Subeditors write their own headlines, so you don't have to agonise over that. What you do need to do is get the gist of the story into the first paragraph, hoping that it's interesting enough for the reporter to read on.

Different elements of the story are presented in a series of short paragraphs: the medieval history; how the school became interested in it; the intention to hurl children into the air again; the village's involvement; and the charity which will benefit from it.

Journalists love quotes, so we've thrown one in, just in case the newsroom is feeling lazy and decides to run the piece as it stands. It's more likely, though, that they'll seize on something to ring the school about – probably the health and safety aspects of child-throwing.

From the clear English point of view, note the absence of obscure words, convoluted thought or any straining for effect. Any of these would be wastefully counter-productive.

A letter of complaint

The danger when you're angry is that you blow your top. That's sometimes productive in a face-to-face confrontation, and it can certainly make you feel better, but once you've written something down and sent it off, you can't retrieve it.

Here's a letter to the headteacher about the persistent bullying your son has had to put up with. There's nothing much worse for a parent than this, and you have no doubt that your fury is justified. Make sure that it's a controlled fury.

Dear Mrs Barleycorn,

I write to complain about the continued bullying that Sam has been subjected to in the first weeks of this half-term.

You will remember that we agreed in December that he should move to a new class in the hope that this would solve the problem. It hasn't.

There have been three incidents in the past week alone. On Monday he was set upon by three other boys, who took his lunch box and scattered the contents around the playground. On Tuesday he was pinched and prodded throughout his maths lesson, and Mr Smith told him not to make a fuss when he complained. On Thursday his jacket was taken from the cloakroom peg, and it was later found, soiled and wet, in the lavatory.

I understand that the school has a 'no blame' policy, but I'm afraid this is most unfair. Sam is a happy boy at home and miserable at school, and this is solely because of other children whose behaviour is allowed to continue unchecked.

Although I am reluctant to take this problem to the governors, I shall have no option unless you can reassure us that measures have been taken to ensure that Sam leads a normal school life. I would be grateful for a swift reply.

Yours sincerely . . .

Mrs Barleycorn can be left in no doubt about either your anger or your determination to make things right for your son, but you have made no outrageous claims that she can turn to her advantage if she wishes to belittle your case.

Your letter is written in plain English and moves logically, and forcefully, to its conclusion. First you state the nature of the letter, to get her in the right frame of mind: it's a complaint. Next, the history. It's not a new problem, and you point out that the potential solution has failed. (That simple 'It hasn't' says it all.)

The third paragraph requires care. Here you set out, in unadorned language and with no more detail than is required, what Sam has gone through: if those are true allegations, nobody can accuse you of exaggeration.

Paragraph four is a protest about the school's bullying policy (you may never agree with Mrs B. about that, but you've a right to your opinion), and the final paragraph is a politely worded threat. Something must be done.

Parents whose level of education is some way below that of a headteacher may feel nervous about writing a letter of this kind, but take a close look at its wording and you'll see that it doesn't demand a fancy vocabulary. Clear English is democratic: don't be afraid to use it.

• *A word about layout:* Reports, newsletters and online posts often use separated paragraphs as on this page, but indented paras with no gaps between are the norm for personal letters.

A newsletter

We all get so much bumf through the post that we readily discard anything that fails to hold our attention. If you're responsible for preparing a members' circular, break everything down into short sections with clear headings.

With a small group you can be personal and even inject some humour, but be wary of taxing your readers' patience with rambling sentences. And, of course, always be aware of the resident peeve who loves to leap on a careless mistake.

Hazelwood Gardening Club
Newsletter no. 67

Congratulations to our talks secretary, Mary Jones, who last week won first prize for her floribunda roses at the county show – a first in that category for any of our members. You can see her proudly showing off her cup (and a brand-new hat) on page 13 of this week's *Gazette*.

Subscriptions
These are now due, and Tom Bright will be pleased to receive cheques for £10 (individuals) or £15 (families). The committee has now held fees at this level for five years.

Help needed

Preparations in the village hall will start from 10 a.m. Friday to be ready for 9 a.m. Saturday. Sheila Swinton (856324) would be grateful for volunteers to carry out the following jobs for the autumn show:

- Putting out trestle tables
- Decorating the hall with floral arrangements
- Erecting our club banner over the entrance
- Organising the rosettes
- Collecting money at the door on Saturday

AGM

Advance notice that our AGM will be held at 7 p.m. on the evening of October 21st.

Note how space-saving those bullet points are. And note that complete sentences aren't always necessary: 'Congratulations to . . .' 'Advance notice that . . .' The verbs are understood.

This is pretty boring for anyone not involved with the club, but it's a no-nonsense presentation of information for your members. Most will be grateful that it's no longer than it needs to be.

Clear English motto: Always think of your readers rather than yourself.

A letter of condolence

Some people find themselves crossing the road rather than deal with the embarrassment of meeting an acquaintance who has recently been bereaved. *What should you say?* This diffidence extends to the written word. It's tempting to buy a card in mournful colours and printed with off-the-peg sentiments rather than attempt to express sympathy in your own words.

But revisit our motto at the foot of the previous page: which would your friend prefer?

We considered euphemisms on page 70, and you won't be surprised to learn that we counsel against fudging the terrible fact of death. After all, even those whose unshakable religious convictions promise them reunion in a world to come will be devastated by the immediate vacancy in their lives. Pretend that it hasn't happened, and they may feel betrayed by what seems to be a lack of empathy.

Brevity is one of our watchwords in this book, and the good news about a letter of condolence is that you really don't need to stray beyond a very few well-chosen paragraphs. The message is simple, and the words should match.

Your letter will, of course, be handwritten, rather than typed.

> Dear Liz,
>
> I was so very sorry to hear of Derek's death, but relieved to hear that he felt no pain at the end.
>
> My memories of him will always take me back to our sunny holidays in Cornwall, when he would flap down to the beach in those enormous sandals, urging everyone to join him in the chilly waves. He was such a humorous force of nature, and so gentle with the children. I shall always be grateful for the way he helped Lorna through that difficult episode in her life.
>
> It's hard to imagine how bereft you must be feeling, but I'm sure the presence of your family will help you through this awful time.
>
> Ron joins me in sending love and sympathy,
>
> Margaret

This is artless, and all the better for it. The idea is not to win an essay prize, but to share grief in all its rawness.

You begin with sorrow and end with understanding, but the important part is what a gift-shop card can't hope to provide – the personal memories at the heart of the letter.

A job application

Pointless verbiage is the prevailing curse of letters written in search of work. What are employers supposed to make of such claims as 'I strive for continual excellence,' 'I believe I am the ideal candidate for this post' or 'I am a forward thinker who will make a positive difference to your team'?

Just imagine writing the opposite (to say that you champion shoddy work, that there are plenty of other people better than you or that taking you on would make no difference whatsoever to the company), and you'll perhaps be able to gauge their weary reaction. This is mere empty wordiness – what a jaundiced American would term 'motherhood and apple pie'. Surely you can do better than that.

Yes, you can. The first thing is to look carefully at the advertisement (if you're replying to one) and to learn as much as you can about the firm you're hoping to join. Think not what *your* needs are, but what kind of person *they* need.

And then realise that you're not writing in order to get the job – that's for later – but to get an interview. They're looking for potential.

82

So does it really matter that you're diligent, imaginative, proactive, a good team player and all the rest? Not if these are nothing but the tired clichés of the business world. Everyone else is spouting identical babble, after all. You have to *show* you have such abilities – and clear, fresh and vital language will help you to do it.

Would they be happy working alongside you? That's a factor easy to overlook – but even the introduction to your letter could ruin your chances. They don't want a pleading child:

It would be the greatest honour to work for a prestigious organisation such as yours.

They don't, on the other hand, want an arrogant bull-at-a-gate type:

Your company has a reputation for quality, but I'm confident it would take greater strides forward under my proven managerial abilities.

And they certainly don't want someone who speaks a strangled form of English:

I am responding to the position as advertised by yourselves in the . . .

Back to our watchwords: simplicity, brevity and the vocabulary and rhythms of normal speech. Recognise the fact that the company holds the cards, but don't be cowed.

Dear Mr Jenkins,

I'm enclosing my CV for the sales director job you have advertised in the trade press.

As you will see, I have experience which broadly fits your needs. What appeals to me about the direction your company plans to take is the emphasis on finding new markets in previously neglected areas. That's something I have been trying to encourage during my time at Grimshaws.

I'm a great believer in promoting staff from within, and if invited for interview I would be pleased to put forward my ideas about training those young recruits who show potential for becoming the managers of the future.

I would be sad to leave Grimshaws, which is a well-run family firm, but I believe your company offers great potential for a sales director with drive and vision.

Yours sincerely . . .

Your CV, if it's well organised, will speak for itself. This covering letter has a different function altogether. Here you give your prospective new employers a hint about how you will help take their company forward if they give you the job.

It may well be that this would be a step up for you, and therefore better paid than your present job, but you have given a more positive reason (from their point of view) for wanting to change. Without spelling it out, you're hinting that you are too dynamic for the rather staid family firm where you work at present. Although you're careful not to sound disloyal, you have ideas that are too advanced for Grimshaws but would be of great benefit here.

Perhaps the staff training paragraph is a response to something you've picked up about the company in your researches, but even if it's just a bee in your bonnet, it reveals that you care about the workforce and may have some useful ideas about staff development.

Self-praise? That 'sales director with drive and vision' could obviously be you, but you've contrived to word this so that you're not making a direct claim. Let's hope they interview you.

Letter of apology 1

'Sorry' can, indeed, be the hardest word. Putting things right face to face is usually the best policy, but sometimes, when personal relationships have almost broken down, the only way to approach the wounded party is by writing a letter.

Here we counsel extreme caution, and advise a draft copy followed by as many revisions as may be necessary. The written word is powerful, and a hastily composed note can cause more trouble than it solves.

First decide the stance you intend to take. If you feel that the blame lies with both parties, tread more carefully than if you plan to admit that you were entirely in the wrong.

We've all heard one kind of public apology which cuts no ice at all. A politician defending his behaviour despite a raft of damning evidence against him will say, 'If I have offended anyone, then I apologise.' Why doesn't this work? Because it's nothing but a poorly disguised attempt to protest his innocence while blaming his 'victim' for being too sensitive. It simply (effective cliché) rubs salt into the wound.

86

Far better, in your letter, to concentrate on what you admit are your own failings. Minor disagreements can be sorted out once you're talking again.

Dear Phoebe,

I've been so miserable since we fell out, and I want to apologise for what I know were unkind and unjustified slurs I made in the heat of the moment.

You well know how impulsive I can be, and I'm sure a whole lot of people have good reason to think I'm just a spoilt brat who always wants her own way. You've always been nice to me, which is why I feel so awful about taking advantage of your kindness.

Can we start again, please? In my mind I've been eating humble pie for the last three weeks, and I'm determined to show you how much I value your friendship. I hope we can meet at Ben's party and perhaps start to put things back together again.

With love,
Carrie

Note that there's no mention of the reason for your outburst. Raise that thorny issue, and Phoebe may well feel obliged to defend herself – and so attack you in the same breath.

Letter of apology 2

Such abject grovelling isn't usually an option for a business, which will have an eye on the financial consequences of admitting failure. But if you're running a company which has made a mistake, you need to apologise with appropriate humility or suffer a justified blow to your reputation.

The equivalent of the politician's 'If I have offended' line is the use of weasel words which qualify your acceptance of blame. When a power failure cuts a customer's supply, it's no comfort whatsoever to be told by the power company – and we've all read this kind of thing – 'It does seem that you may have suffered a temporary inconvenience, suggesting that we perhaps fell somewhat below the high standards we set ourselves.'

What we have there is an audacious 'may have', as if the problem has possibly been invented, a down-playing of the customer's grief ('a temporary inconvenience') and an uncalled-for boast (those 'high standards').

Reading between the lines of this offensive stuff is evidently easier than writing honest English.

Here's a suggested letter from a small building firm to a client with a leaking roof.

Dear Mr Roberts,

I am very sorry to hear that your new extension roof has developed a leak. I can't, of course, diagnose the problem without an inspection, but you clearly shouldn't be experiencing any trouble with it so soon after the building work has been completed.

You have asked us to make any necessary repairs at the beginning of next week, and I can assure you that I shall be there myself in order to make sure that our team sorts it out swiftly.

Please accept my apologies for the inconvenience this has caused you.

Yours sincerely . . .

It would be tempting to begin by expressing 'surprise' at receiving the complaint, but this carries a subliminal 'surely not!' message, as if you don't entirely trust the client. Tempting, too, to refer to the roofing material, which is made by a supplier, but don't do that: you fitted it and so you're responsible.

And don't for a second think of writing 'any inconvenience', as if it may be a trivial matter after all. It certainly *has* caused the householder inconvenience, if measured only in irritation, and you need to face up to that.

Note that you haven't laid yourself open to any costs other than the repair – if it is indeed your fault rather than his.

Dear John/Jane

Perhaps, on second thoughts, 'goodbye' is even harder to say than 'sorry'. The relationship has come to an end – as far as you're concerned, at least – and you need a form of words to soften the blow while at the same time making it clear that the rift is permanent.

We assume that there's been no falling out between you, only a lowering of the emotional temperature. You want to escape.

Dear John/Jane,
I don't know whether you've been expecting this letter, because I'm aware that I've been rather quiet and withdrawn lately. I just feel that we've gone as far as we can together and that it's time for us both to make a new start.

I don't want you to think that I haven't enjoyed this last year. We've had some lovely times, haven't we? Our Norfolk Broads holiday will stay in my memory for ever, and we've always enjoyed those walks by the river.

Let's please be friends again once we've got over the pain of the break. It hurts me, but I've thought about it a great deal and I'm sure it's the right thing to do.

> With love,
> Jane/John

And e-finally . . .

Would you send the above letter as an e-message rather than handwritten in an envelope? That probably depends on your age. We of the older generation shudder to think of intimacies exchanged so casually, especially as it's easy to hit the 'send' key with scarcely a moment's reflection.

The Internet will gradually develop its own etiquette, but we'd argue that most of the advice in these pages is relevant to the e-world. In that often shambolically democratic universe, those with a mastery of the language will always have an advantage over those who stumble.

If you apply for a job using the Internet, be sure that your use of language will be judged every bit as severely as if you'd sent a letter in the post. Similarly, if you venture into the blogosphere, don't expect to make much of an impact unless you've learned how to develop a logical argument in effectively competent English.

There is, though, a less obvious yet immensely satisfying reward in prospect. As you refine your control over the nuts and bolts of your mother tongue, you'll improve not only the clarity of what you write but (the two go together) the clarity of your thinking.

Happy (clear) scribbling!

Glossary

active voice The most common way of constructing a sentence, in which the subject carries out the action described by the verb.

adjective A 'describing word' used to give information about a noun or pronoun.

adverb A 'describing word' used with a verb to describe how an action is done. Most English adverbs end in *-ly*.

apostrophe A little mark (') with two chief functions: to mark missing letters, as in *don't* and *shan't*; and to indicate possession, as in *Tom's books*. It is sometimes also used to show plurals (*P's and Q's*) in forms which are not part of standard English usage.

conjunction A linking word, such as *and, or, but, yet* or *while*.

infinitive The basic form of a verb, usually preceded by *to*.

noun A 'naming word' referring to a person, thing, place or idea.

object The person or thing to which the action described by the verb is done.

paragraph A self-contained group of sentences which together deal with a single idea.

parenthesis A phrase inserted into a sentence (between brackets or dashes) to give additional information.

passive voice A grammatical construction in which the noun that would be the object of an active sentence

(*Spurs trounced Arsenal*) becomes the subject (*Arsenal were trounced by Spurs*).

preposition A word such as *at, in, by, down* or *under*, which expresses the relationship of a noun or pronoun to some other person, thing or action in the sentence.

present participle The form of the verb, ending in *-ing*, that also functions as an adjective.

register The appropriate tone of voice to reflect the intended audience of a piece of writing.

sentence A sequence of words, consisting of at least a subject and a verb, which stands by itself as a statement or question.

structure In writing, the organisation of ideas in a logical way to develop an argument.

subject The person or thing that carries out the action described by the verb.

tense The form of a verb indicating when (past, present, future) the action takes place.

verb A 'doing word' that names an action.